I0816949

BEST OF
MARCH
MADNESS

ICONIC MARCH MADNESS CHAMPIONS

BY CHARLIE BEATTIE

abdobooks.com

Published by Abdo Publishing, a division of ABDO, PO Box 398166, Minneapolis, Minnesota 55439.

Printed in the United States of America, North Mankato, Minnesota.
102025
012026

Cover Photos: Winslow Townson/AP Images, AP Images, Andy Lyons/Getty Images Sport/Getty Images
Interior Photos: Tyler Schank/NCAA Photos/Getty Images, 4–5; Anthony Neste/Sports Illustrated/Getty Images, 7; Christian Petersen/Getty Images Sport/Getty Images, 9; Bettmann/Getty Images, 10–11; Rich Clarkson/Sports Illustrated/Getty Images, 13; Focus On Sport/Getty Images, 14, 25; Rich Clarkson/NCAA Photos/Getty Images, 16, 45; Gary Mook/Allsport/Getty Images Sport/Getty Images, 19; John G. Zimmerman/Sports Illustrated/Getty Images, 20–21; Rick Stewart/Hulton Archive/Getty Images, 23; Damian Strohmeyer/Allsport/Hulton Archive/Getty Images, 27; Jonathan Daniel/Getty Images Sport/Getty Images, 28–29; Brian Bahr/Allsport/Getty Images Sport/Getty Images, 30; Patrick Schneider/Charlotte Observer/Tribune News Service/Getty Images, 33; Rich Sugg/Kansas City Star/Tribune News Service/Getty Images, 34; Bob Stowell/Robert W. Stowell Jr./Archive Photos/Getty Images, 36–37; Wade Payne/AP Images, 39; Jamie Schwaberow/NCAA Photos/Getty Images, 40; Justin Tafoya/NCAA Photos/Getty Images, 43

Editor: Dalton Rains
Series Designer: Ebonee Estrella

Library of Congress Control Number: 2025939196

Publisher's Cataloging-in-Publication Data

Names: Beattie, Charlie, author.
Title: Iconic March Madness champions / by Charlie Beattie
Description: Minneapolis, Minnesota: Abdo Publishing, 2026 | Series: Best of March Madness | Includes online resources and index.
Identifiers: ISBN 9781098298166 (lib. bdg.) | ISBN 9798384931966 (ebook)
Subjects: LCSH: Basketball--Juvenile literature. | College sports--Juvenile literature. | Basketball--Tournaments--United States--Juvenile literature. | College sports--United States--History--Juvenile literature. | NCAA Basketball Tournament--Juvenile literature. | March Madness (National Collegiate Athletic Association)--Juvenile literature.
Classification: DDC 796.32363--dc23

TABLE OF CONTENTS

PURDUE
15
CLINGAN
32
KARABAN
11

CHAPTER ONE

JOINING THE BLUE BLOODS

More than 74,000 fans in Glendale, Arizona, looked on as the University of Connecticut (UConn) Huskies took the court. Nearly 15 million more people watched on TV. The team was playing in the final of the 2024 National Collegiate Athletics Association (NCAA) men's basketball tournament. Everyone wanted to see whether the defending champion Huskies could get past Purdue. Winning back-to-back titles had become a rare feat over the years. Since 1973, only two schools had pulled it off. UConn hoped to become the third.

There was even more history at stake for UConn. The Huskies had reached their first Final Four only 30 years earlier. Since then, UConn had piled up five championships. Both Duke and Indiana also owned

UConn and Purdue were both No. 1 seeds in the 2024 men's NCAA Tournament.

five titles. The Huskies were on the verge of passing those storied programs and moving into a tie for the third-most national championships of all time. For a school that had long battled for respect, a victory would silence any doubters.

A MODERN DYNASTY

College men's basketball has long been ruled by so-called "blue blood" programs. Schools such as Indiana, Kentucky, North Carolina, and the University of California, Los Angeles (UCLA), have each won multiple championships. These teams regularly contend for more. For decades, UConn was nowhere near that list.

The Huskies' luck began to change in 1986. That year, Jim Calhoun became UConn's head coach. Calhoun had already built a strong résumé at Northeastern. He believed in hard work, both on and off the court. As his teams battled to improve throughout the 1990s, Calhoun hustled on the recruiting trail. He worked to bring top talents to UConn.

After years of coming up short in the NCAA Tournament, the Huskies finally reached the title game in 1999. There, they were heavy underdogs against Duke. The Blue Devils had won back-to-back titles only 10 years before. But Calhoun's up-and-coming Huskies outlasted the respected program. UConn won 77–74.

The 1987–88 Huskies improved to 20–14 just one season after the team finished 9–19.

Calhoun had taken the Huskies to the top, and he worked hard to keep them there. In 2004, he led UConn to another title run. This time, the Huskies downed Georgia Tech 82–73 in the championship game. In 2011, UConn beat Butler for its third title. One year later, with the program on solid ground, Calhoun retired. Former UConn point guard Kevin Ollie took over for the 2012–13 season. In 2014, the No. 7 seed Huskies shocked the field by winning yet another championship. That gave them more titles than the historic powerhouse Kansas Jayhawks.

BACK-TO-BACK

Despite the team's success, UConn still felt overlooked as a top program. In 2018, coach Dan Hurley took over from Ollie. After a few years of struggle, Hurley and the Huskies entered the 2023 tournament as a No. 4 seed. From there, the energetic, unselfish team destroyed the competition. UConn easily won all six of its games, including a 76–59 rout of San Diego State in the title game. Afterward, Hurley said, "[Our] blood is as blue as can be."

Hurley knew that it wouldn't be easy to win back-to-back titles. College basketball changed a lot in the 2020s. Players were allowed to switch schools as often as they liked. The lineups of many teams changed a lot from year to year. But Hurley managed to keep his Huskies together. Led by familiar faces, including 7-foot-2 center Donovan Clingan, UConn went into the 2024 tournament with a 31–3 record and a top seed.

The Huskies cruised to the title game. There, they faced a 34–4 Purdue team. The Boilermakers boasted Zach Edey, a two-time winner of the Naismith Trophy as the nation's best player. Purdue's towering 7-foot-4 center was the biggest star on the court, but the Huskies knew a full-team effort could bring another title to Connecticut. That's exactly what happened. Of UConn's 30 baskets, 18 came after assists. One of those assists came early in

UConn guard Tristen Newton (2) scored 20 points in the 2024 title game.

the second half. With UConn leading 43–34, point guard Tristen Newton and forward Samson Johnson executed a perfect pick-and-roll. Newton fed Johnson for an alley-oop dunk. It electrified the crowd and gave UConn a double-digit lead.

The Huskies never looked back. They pulled away for a 75–60 victory and became the first team in 17 years to win back-to-back championships. With a sixth title, UConn trailed only Kentucky and UCLA in all-time championships. Now, no one could doubt the color of the program's blood.

KENTUCKY
15
KENTUCKY
HANK LUISETTI DIAGRAM BOARD

CHAPTER TWO

LEGENDS OF THE GAME

Confidence was never an issue for Adolph Rupp. In 1930, he was still coaching high school basketball when he interviewed for the men's head coaching job at Kentucky. Despite having yet to coach a single college game, Rupp told the interviewers that he was the best coach in the country.

Nearly two decades later, many fans agreed with that claim. The legendary coach never had a losing season. Rupp liked fast-paced basketball. Speedy play helped his team blow away the competition. In 1948, he took a 33–3 Wildcats team into the NCAA Tournament. Kentucky first beat Columbia and Holy Cross. Then the Wildcats dominated Baylor 58–42 in the championship game. Rupp began calling his starting lineup "The Fabulous Five."

Adolph Rupp, *left*, was Kentucky's head coach from 1930 to 1972.

Four of Rupp's five starters were back for the next season. Kentucky reached the title game once again. Rupp squared off with another legendary coach. Hank Iba's Oklahoma A&M teams had won back-to-back NCAA Tournaments in 1945 and 1946. Both coaches had grand nicknames. Iba was known as "The Iron Duke of Defense." Kentucky fans called Rupp "The Baron of the Bluegrass."

Iba's defensive team slowed down the pace of the game, but Rupp's Wildcats still pulled away for a 46–36 victory. Kentucky's star center, Alex Groza, put up 25 points in the victory. After the team returned home, 25,000 fans gathered to celebrate.

Rupp captured a third title in 1951. A few years later, the coach got a chance for a fourth. In 1958, Kentucky's roster of flashy players drove the ultra-disciplined Rupp crazy. Some fans now called the starters "The Fiddlin' Five" because of their frustrating mistakes. But even those mistakes couldn't hold back the talented players. They powered through the 1958 tournament. The national championship was a matchup with Seattle. Wildcats guard Vernon Hatton scored 30 points in the 1958 title game. Kentucky topped Seattle 84–72. It was Rupp's final title, but his dominant teams had helped make the NCAA Tournament a popular event. The Baron of the Bluegrass set the tone for every college basketball dynasty that followed.

THE WIZARD OF WESTWOOD

The UCLA Bruins and Duke Blue Devils raced up and down the court. But as the fast-paced 1964 title game wore on, Duke's players wore out. John Wooden's Bruins kept pressing. Eventually, UCLA put together a 16–0 run. The Bruins pulled away to win 98–83.

Wooden's first championship kick-started one of the greatest dynasties in American sports. Led by shooting guard Gail Goodrich's 42 points, UCLA repeated the next year with a 91–80 victory over Michigan. The Bruins missed the tournament in 1966, but everyone knew

During John Wooden's time at UCLA, the Bruins went 620–147.

UCLA center Lew Alcindor (33), later known as Kareem Abul-Jabbar, averaged 26.2 points per game in 1967–68.

Wooden's team would be back. At the time, freshmen weren't eligible to play for varsity teams. They had to play on freshman teams while they waited their turn. In 1966, UCLA's freshman team featured 7-foot, 2-inch center Lew Alcindor.

Alcindor, who later changed his name to Kareem Abdul-Jabbar, was a defensive powerhouse. His freshman squad even beat the varsity team in an exhibition game.

As soon as Alcindor joined varsity, the Bruins became nearly unstoppable. The gangly center averaged 29.0 points and 15.5 rebounds per game in the 1966–67 season. UCLA went 30–0 and beat Dayton 79–64 in the championship game.

Between the 1966–67 and 1972–73 seasons, the Bruins lost only five games. They won the NCAA title every year. UCLA wore down opponents with relentless pressure on defense. On offense, Wooden stressed quick ball movement. He became known as "The Wizard of Westwood" after the neighborhood where UCLA is located.

The quiet and modest Wooden didn't care for his nickname. While many basketball coaches are loud and excited on the bench, Wooden usually looked calm. But he was definitely in charge. He just didn't like flashiness. Wooden didn't even want his players dribbling between their legs. He thought it was unnecessary.

In 1973–74, star center Bill Walton led the Bruins to a 30–0 record and a title. But the strict Wooden didn't loosen up on the rules. Before the next season, Walton showed up to practice with long hair and a beard. Wooden told his player to get rid of both. Walton refused, saying it was his right to express himself. Wooden agreed, but coolly responded that it was his right as a coach to pick who played. Walton cut his hair.

Center Bill Walton (32) won three Naismith Trophies with UCLA.

UCLA's seven-year championship streak was snapped in the 1974 national semifinals. But the Bruins returned a year later. They survived a 75–74 overtime nail-biter to reach the title game. There, they took on Kentucky.

Adolph Rupp had retired three years earlier, but the Wildcats were still a top team under coach Joe B. Hall. The matchup between two of college basketball's most successful schools didn't disappoint fans. Four of UCLA's starters played every minute of the fast-paced game.

Led by forward Richard Washington's 28 points, the Bruins pulled away late to win 92–85. After the game, Wooden decided to retire on top. In the following decades, no other men's college basketball dynasty came close to Wooden's success.

PURSUIT OF PERFECTION

Another team entered the 1975 NCAA Tournament with high hopes. Coach Bobby Knight's Indiana Hoosiers went into the tournament with a 29–0 record. However, the team ran headfirst into Kentucky in the regional final. Indiana's star forward, Scott May, was dealing with an injury. He had to leave the game early. Kentucky won 92–90 on the way to its championship matchup against UCLA.

Indiana was even more motivated during the 1975–76 season. Perfection was the goal. Heading into the national semifinals, the 30–0 Hoosiers were on track. They took down UCLA 65–51.

Indiana's win set up a championship meeting with Big Ten Conference rival Michigan. The Hoosiers had beaten the Wolverines twice during the season. But Michigan played a physical first half. At halftime, Indiana headed into the locker room trailing 35–29. Even worse, another star player was injured. Point guard Bobby Wilkerson had left the game with a concussion.

Indiana's players cursed their bad luck as they waited for their coach to enter the locker room. They were also worried that Knight might scream at them. He was one of college basketball's all-time yellers. But the coach surprised them. He calmly told his players that they were throwing away a chance at a perfect season.

Inspired, the Hoosiers hammered Michigan in the second half. A healthy May led all scorers with 26 points. Center Kent Benson added 25. Indiana won 86–68 for its first title since 1953. The Hoosiers were the seventh undefeated champion since 1956, but in the coming decades, no other team matched the feat.

DONNING THE CROWN

In the mid-1950s, the University of San Francisco put together an incredible two-season run. Star center Bill Russell led the Dons to back-to-back championships in 1955 and 1956. In 1956, the 29–0 team became the first NCAA title winner with a perfect record.

Bobby Knight coached at Indiana for 29 years. The Hoosiers won three national championships during that time.

CHAPTER THREE

PIONEERING WOMEN'S PROGRAMS

Women's college basketball teams existed for nearly the entire history of the sport, but women didn't begin playing for a national championship until 1972. At the time, the tournament was overseen by the Association of Intercollegiate Athletics for Women (AIAW).

Several teams became powerhouses during the AIAW era. Immaculata College, a tiny school in Pennsylvania, won the first three titles. Between 1975 and 1977, Delta State in Mississippi also completed a three-peat.

The women's game didn't get much attention. Few fans noticed these early titles. That didn't change

Lusia Harris, *in black*, averaged 25.9 points per game during her time at Delta State in the mid-1970s.

much even after the NCAA began its own women's tournament in 1982. A sellout crowd of 9,531 showed up to the final in Norfolk, Virginia. But many had been given free tickets. They watched 35–1 Louisiana Tech knock off Cheyney 76–62.

THE WOMEN OF TROY

In 1983, Louisiana Tech faced a flashy challenger in the national championship. The University of Southern California (USC) Trojans had a 30–2 record. The team's frontcourt boasted high-scoring twin sisters Paula and Pam McGee. But USC's biggest star was Cheryl Miller. Ever since scoring 105 points in a high school game, the freshman forward had been a national phenomenon. Miller had a fierce drive to win. Her smooth shooting form and shot-blocking abilities took the college game by storm.

Miller scored a game-high 27 points in the 1983 title game, but the tight contest came down to a defensive stand. With 14 seconds left, USC led 69–67. A Trojan drove to the basket. Then Louisiana Tech point guard Kim Mulkey poked the ball away. A teammate grabbed it and passed it back to Mulkey, who drove to the opposite basket. Just in time, USC guard Cynthia Cooper stepped into Mulkey's path and drew a charge. USC hung on for the victory.

Forward Cheryl Miller (31) scored 3,018 points in her four years with USC.

It was only the beginning for "The Women of Troy." The next year, USC faced the Tennessee Lady Volunteers in the title game. Miller turned it on after halftime. She finished the game with 16 points and seven assists. USC outscored Tennessee 46–33 in the second half to win 72–61. The NCAA had its first women's basketball dynasty.

VOLUNTEER VICTORIES

By the 1987 women's NCAA Tournament, Pat Summitt had been coaching Tennessee for 13 years. Summitt was an intense coach. She demanded a lot from her players. When a Lady Volunteer made a mistake on the court, she was often met with a glare from the coach. Players called the intense look "The Summitt Stare." Behind the scenes, Summitt had a gentler side. She took a deep interest in players' well-being and personal growth. Both sides of Summitt's coaching style paid off. Between 1982 and 1986, she led Tennessee to three Final Four appearances. However, the Lady Vols could never finish on top.

Tennessee made yet another run in the 1987 NCAA Tournament. Summitt and the Lady Vols cruised all the way to the title game. They were the underdogs in the matchup against Louisiana Tech. Summitt spent long nights designing a rugged defense to take on Louisiana Tech's powerful inside game. The preparation paid off. Tennessee cruised to a 67–44 victory.

Summitt was an excellent recruiter. Her teams were usually stocked with the top talents in the country. Point guard Tonya Edwards and forward Bridgette Gordon led the team's 1987 championship run. Much to the dismay of opposing coaches, both members of the dynamic duo were still around two years later.

Tennessee was the No. 1 team in the country through the 1988–89 season, but the team's road to a title got bumpier when Edwards injured her knee midway through the year. That meant Gordon had to carry the team. The powerful forward was ready for the challenge. She recorded 24 points and 8 rebounds in a Final Four

Tennessee forward Bridgette Gordon (30) averaged 16.4 points per game in 1986–87.

matchup against Maryland. After that, the Lady Vols faced the undefeated Auburn Tigers in the championship game. It was a back-and-forth game, but Gordon took over late. Tennessee pulled away for a 76–60 win. Summitt led the team to yet another title in 1991, making sure the Lady Vols remained a top force in women's basketball.

CARDINAL RULES

By the mid-1980s, coach Tara VanDerveer had turned Ohio State into a nationally ranked team. Then she surprised everyone. VanDerveer left the Buckeyes for Stanford. Many people thought the move was a mistake. The year before she arrived, Stanford had gone just 9–19.

VanDerveer and the Cardinal finished the 1985–86 season with a losing record. The team missed the NCAA Tournament again in 1986–87. Things looked bleak, but VanDerveer kept at it. She taught her players the complicated triangle offense. It was the same strategy the Chicago Bulls used to win six National Basketball Association (NBA) titles in the 1990s. VanDerveer's recruiting skills also started to pay off. Better players kept trickling in, including shooting guard Jennifer Azzi and forward Katy Steding. Stanford entered the 1989–90 season with high hopes. The confident players even hung up signs in the locker room that read: "Get comfortable with it. 1990 National Champions."

TOUGH-LUCK TIGERS

The Auburn Tigers came very close to forming their own dynasty in the late 1980s and early 1990s. In 1988, the Tigers lost the championship game 56–54 to Louisiana Tech. A year later, Auburn fell 76–60 in the title game to Tennessee. Then in 1990, the Tigers lost 88–81 to Stanford after leading by as many as nine points early in the game. In those three seasons, Auburn had a combined record of 92–12.

Both Azzi and Steding were sharpshooters from three-point range. They led Stanford to a 1990 title matchup against Auburn. There, VanDerveer turned her shooters loose. Steding made six shots from beyond the arc. Azzi added four more. Point guard Sonja Henning outscored them both, though. She finished the game with 21 points. Stanford won 88–81.

The win was the start of an amazing coaching run. VanDerveer coached at Stanford until 2024. She won two more titles in that time.

Stanford point guard Sonja Henning averaged 8.8 points and 6.7 assists per game in 1989–90.

DUKE
32
HOWARD
25

CHAPTER FOUR

A NEW ERA

Duke faced off with the University of Nevada, Las Vegas (UNLV), in the 1991 men's Final Four. Few fans thought the Blue Devils could win. A year before, the two teams had met in the championship. In that game, the Runnin' Rebels blew out Duke 103–73. It was the biggest title-game rout in men's tournament history.

UNLV entered the rematch with an undefeated record. But Duke hung in the game behind its trio of standouts. Freshman forward Grant Hill mixed high-rising dunks with smooth jump shots. Meanwhile, sophomore point guard Bobby Hurley was on his way to becoming the all-time men's basketball assists leader. But the team's heartbeat was multitalented Christian Laettner. The 6-foot-11 center was a strong shooter and a physical rebounder. He also carried himself with a confident air that frustrated opponents.

Center Christian Laettner (32) played at Duke from 1988–89 to 1991–92.

Mike Krzyzewski ended his coaching career with 1,202 wins.

Laettner mixed low-post moves with well-timed jumpers against UNLV. He finished the Final Four matchup with 28 points in a shocking 79–77 Duke win. Two days later, the Blue Devils took down Kansas 72–65 to win their first championship.

COACH K

Duke's 1991 title win ushered in an era of greatness. In 1980, the school had hired little-known Mike Krzyzewski. Duke struggled through "Coach K's" first few seasons. Many die-hard Duke fans even wanted him fired. But Coach K wasn't discouraged. In 1986, the Blue Devils reached the Final Four. That began a run of five straight semifinal appearances.

That streak was under threat in the 1992 Elite Eight. With 2.1 seconds left in overtime, No. 1 seed Duke trailed the Kentucky Wildcats 103–102. The Blue Devils had to go the length of the floor to win. Coach K called a timeout.

Coach K knew that Laettner could make the shot. But first, Duke had to get the ball into shooting range. That meant a long pass. The legendary coach turned to Hill and asked if he could get Laettner the ball. The sophomore nodded. Hill, inbounding the ball from the other end of the court, delivered a 75-foot strike. Laettner caught the ball with his back to the basket and faked to one side. Then he turned back and shot over a defender. The ball dropped through the net as the buzzer sounded. It was one of the NCAA Tournament's most memorable moments.

A week later, Duke took down Michigan 71–51 to become the first back-to-back champion since UCLA in 1973. Coach K was Duke's savior, and he was far from finished. He stayed at Duke until 2022. In that time, he became the sport's all-time wins leader and led the Blue Devils to three more championships.

GATORS CHOMP

Through the early 2000s, the men's NCAA Tournament was still dominated by a handful of teams. Blue bloods frequently contended for the national title. But in 2006 and 2007, a school better known as a football powerhouse took over the hardwood.

Billy Donovan became the Florida Gators' head coach in 1996. Donovan had been an assistant at Kentucky in the early 1990s. He brought Kentucky's winning attitude to his new team. A surprise run to the 2000 national championship game showed that the Gators were on the rise. Six years later, Donovan hoped for another run. Florida was a tough, balanced team filled with young players. Point guard Taurean Green dished out passes to big men Corey Brewer, Al Horford, and Joakim Noah. All four players were sophomores.

Noah signified Florida's hardworking nature. The son of a former professional tennis player, Noah defended the lane with ferocity. The long-haired center often celebrated with wild howls. Florida rode his intensity through the 2006 NCAA Tournament. None of the Gators' six opponents scored more than 62 points. Noah dominated UCLA in the championship game. He piled up 16 points and nine rebounds, leading Florida to a 73–57 win.

In 2006–07, a familiar starting lineup led Florida back to the tournament. Led by their four junior stars, the Gators looked like the team to beat. They played like it too. They won their first five tournament games by eight points or more. Then they moved on to a championship

Florida center Joakim Noah (13) had six blocks in the 2006 title game.

battle against Ohio State. A few months earlier, Florida's football team had blown out the Buckeyes to win the national title. The basketball team made it two titles in three months. Behind a balanced scoring attack, Florida won 84–75.

ONE-AND-DONE DYNASTIES

Florida's returning starters made the Gators something of a rarity in college basketball. By the late 2000s, many top players stayed in school only one season before moving to the NBA. That made it even more important to recruit great players every year. During the 2010s, many of these

THE UNTOUCHABLES

Many fans consider the 1996 Kentucky Wildcats the most talented team to ever win the men's NCAA Tournament. Coach Rick Pitino's roster featured nine future NBA players. Known as "The Untouchables," the Wildcats won four of their six NCAA Tournament games by 20 points or more. They finished the dominant run by knocking off Syracuse 76–67 to clinch the title.

top recruits joined coach John Calipari at Kentucky. In 2011–12, six of Calipari's top seven scorers were either freshmen or sophomores. Forward Anthony Davis had been the top recruit in high school. As a freshman, he led the young Wildcats to a 38–2 record. They knocked off Kansas 67–59 in that season's title game.

Meanwhile, other teams proved that they could still win with experienced players. Going into the 2015–16 season, the Villanova Wildcats hadn't won a title since 1985. But coach Jay Wright had a team filled with juniors and seniors. In a tense final with North Carolina, that experience paid off. The Tar Heels tied the game with seconds left. But Wildcats forward Kris Jenkins answered with a three-pointer at the buzzer to capture a 77–74 victory.

Kentucky forward Anthony Davis (23) averaged 4.7 blocks per game in 2011–12.

Two years later, Wright's Villanova team didn't need late-game heroics. The Wildcats led the nation with an average of 86.6 points per game. In the NCAA Tournament, they won every game by at least 12 points. They capped the run by routing Michigan 79–62 in the championship game.

CONNECTICU
50

CHAPTER FIVE

TOP OF THEIR GAME

When Geno Auriemma took over UConn's women's basketball team in 1985, the school had only ever had one winning season. Auriemma used his savvy recruiting skills to build up the program. By 1994–95, Auriemma had assembled a talented squad. Rebecca Lobo and Kara Wolters formed a fierce inside combo. Nykesha Sales and Jennifer Rizzotti were among the country's top guards. The Huskies rolled into the Final Four with a 33–0 record while averaging 89.5 points per game.

To complete its perfect season, UConn had to beat both Tara VanDerveer's Stanford and Pat Summitt's Tennessee. The Huskies knocked out the Cardinal 87–60 in the Final Four. With just under two minutes left in the championship game, UConn and Tennessee

UConn forward and center Rebecca Lobo (50) won the Naismith Trophy for the 1994–95 season.

were tied 61–61. Rizzotti grabbed a long rebound and sprinted down the court. She avoided a Tennessee defender with a crafty crossover dribble. Then she put UConn up for good with a left-handed layup. The Huskies won 70–64.

TENNESSEE THREE

Despite Tennessee's 1995 championship-game loss, Summitt wasn't about to give up the women's basketball crown for good. The following season, the Lady Volunteers knocked out UConn 88–83 in overtime in the Final Four. Tennessee then topped Georgia 83–65 for Summitt's fourth national title. A year later, star forward Chamique Holdsclaw put up 24 points in a 68–59 championship-game win over Old Dominion.

With Holdsclaw back for the 1998 tournament, Tennessee looked unbeatable. The Lady Vols capped off a 39–0 season with two dominant performances. They first smashed Arkansas 86–58 in the Final Four. Then they beat Louisiana Tech 93–75 in the championship. That made Tennessee the first women's team to win three straight titles.

HUSKIES HEAVEN

By 2000, the rivalry between Tennessee and UConn dominated women's college basketball. The teams battled for top recruits. They also played a highly anticipated mid-season game each year. One of the teams was almost always ranked No. 1. Off the court, coaches Summitt and Auriemma frequently sparred in the media. Auriemma once called Tennessee "the evil empire." Meanwhile, according to Auriemma, Summitt accused UConn of breaking recruiting rules.

Tennessee knocked the Huskies out of the tournament in both 1996 and 1997. In 2000, UConn was out for revenge. The teams were both No. 1 seeds and met in the title game. UConn shut down Tennessee stars Semeka Randall and Tamika Catchings. The Huskies captured their second title with a lopsided 71–52 victory.

Tennessee coach Pat Summitt, *left*, and UConn coach Geno Auriemma both led their teams to more than 1,000 wins.

Forward Candace Parker celebrates Tennessee's 2007 national championship victory.

The rivals' next big showdown came in the 2002 Final Four. The 37–0 Huskies featured a three-guard lineup of Sue Bird, Swin Cash, and Diana Taurasi. Four of the team's starters averaged 14 points per game. UConn smothered the Lady Volunteers 79–56. Afterward, Summitt came into UConn's locker room and told them just how good she thought they were. Setting aside the rivalry, she told the Huskies to go and win the title. The team did just that, capping off a perfect 39–0 season with an 82–70 win over Oklahoma.

UConn didn't slow down in 2003 or 2004. With Taurasi leading the way, the Huskies completed a three-peat. They beat Tennessee in both championship games.

SUMMITT AND PARKER

Just when she seemed to fall behind Auriemma in the battle for top recruits, Summitt snagged another star. Candace Parker joined the Lady Volunteers in 2005. By the 2007 NCAA Tournament, other coaches were calling her the best player in the world. The forward led the Lady Vols to a 33–3 record entering that year's title game against Rutgers. She battled through heavy defensive pressure to score 17 points, helping the Lady Vols get back on top with a 59–46 win.

Parker and Summitt weren't finished. In the 2008 title game against Stanford, Parker once again put up 17 points. She also added nine rebounds and four steals. Tennessee won 64–48. Summit retired a few years later.

TWO STREAKS

UConn's 2008 NCAA Tournament run ended at the Final Four. It was only a temporary setback for Auriemma's team. Starting in the fall of 2008, Connecticut didn't lose a game for two years. With forward Maya Moore and center Tina Charles leading the way, UConn put up back-to-back 39–0 seasons and won two more titles.

In the 2009 championship game, Charles hit 11 of 13 shots from the floor and scored 25 points. She also pulled in 19 rebounds in a 76–54 blowout against Louisville. A year later, Moore's 23 points and 11 rebounds

PECK'S PRESENT

In 1999, Purdue knocked off Duke 62–45 to win the women's national title. Boilermakers coach Carolyn Peck became the first Black coach to win a women's championship. Peck saved a strand of the net and gave it to Dawn Staley as a gift, telling Staley to hold on to it until she won one of her own. Staley still had the gift when she led South Carolina to the 2017 title.

guided UConn past Stanford 53–47 in the championship game. UConn eventually won 90 straight games. That broke the NCAA record of 88, set by the UCLA men's team between 1971 and 1974.

The Huskies' next championship run came in 2013. The team won five tournament games to take the title. In the championship, freshman forward Breanna Stewart scorched Louisville with 23 points and nine rebounds.

The Huskies' second game of 2014–15 ended with an overtime loss to Stanford. It turned out to be UConn's only loss of the season. The team cruised through the tournament and won the title. The next season, the Huskies didn't lose a game and became the first women's basketball team to win four titles in a row. UConn rolled to a record-smashing 111-game winning streak. It didn't end until Mississippi State scored on a last-second shot to upset the Huskies in the 2017 Final Four.

A NEW CHALLENGER

In 2008, Dawn Staley became the head coach of a struggling South Carolina team. As Staley built up trust with her team, South Carolina improved. In 2015, the Gamecocks even made a run to the Final Four.

Staley continued to add elite players to the roster. A'ja Wilson, a 6-foot-5-inch forward, dominated Mississippi State in the 2017 championship game. She finished with 23 points and 10 rebounds as South Carolina won 67–55.

Staley's Gamecocks led a wave of new powerhouse teams. South Carolina captured another title in 2022 and a third in 2024, showing there was always room for another team at the top of the women's game.

A'ja Wilson (22) swatted four shots in the 2017 title game.

HONORABLE MENTIONS

MEN

CINCINNATI

Before UCLA came along, the Cincinnati Bearcats were the dynasty of the 1960s. The team beat Ohio State for both the 1961 and 1962 titles. Cincinnati nearly made it three in a row, only to be beaten by Loyola University Chicago on a tip-in at the buzzer in the 1963 championship.

GEORGETOWN

In 1984, star center Patrick Ewing led a dominant Georgetown team to an 84–75 victory over Houston in the championship game. Georgetown coach John Thompson Jr. made history as the first Black coach to win a national title. It was the high point of an incredible four-year run for the Hoyas. They also reached the title game in 1982 and 1985, losing close games each time.

Larry Johnson

UNLV

From the late 1970s to the early 1990s, coach Jerry Tarkanian built a dynasty in the deserts of Nevada. "Tark the Shark's" UNLV teams lived up to their Runnin' Rebel nickname. They played fast-paced offense and high-pressure defense. Tarkanian took the team to the Final Four in 1977 and again in 1987. UNLV finally won it all in 1990 behind powerful forward Larry Johnson. A year later, a 79–77 loss to Duke in the Final Four kept Tarkanian from a shot at back-to-back titles.

WOMEN

TEXAS

In 1986, Jody Conradt's team became the first in NCAA women's basketball to finish a season undefeated. The Longhorns clinched that milestone by frustrating Cheryl Miller and the USC Trojans in the title game.

Brittney Griner

BAYLOR

Towering center Brittney Griner was a one-person wrecking crew for the Baylor Bears. In 2011–12, she averaged 5.2 blocks per game in addition to leading the team in scoring and rebounding. Griner had 26 points, 13 rebounds, and five blocks in an 80–61 championship-game rout of Notre Dame. With the win, Baylor became the first team to finish a season with a 40–0 record.

NOTRE DAME

Notre Dame won its first title under coach Muffet McGraw in 2001. The Fighting Irish then waited 17 years to add another, which they did by beating Mississippi State in 2018. In between, McGraw's teams had their hearts broken in four different title games.

GLOSSARY

assist
A pass that leads directly to a basket.

concussion
A brain injury caused by a blow to the head or a violent shaking of the head and body.

conference
A group of schools that join together to create a league for their sports teams.

contend
To have a good chance at winning a championship.

dynasty
A team that has an extended period of success, usually winning multiple championships in the process.

low-post
The area of the court closest to the basket.

modest
Not overly confident or proud.

overtime
An extra period of play when the score is tied after regulation.

pick-and-roll
A play in which one player sets a screen and rolls toward the basket.

recruit
To try to convince a high school athlete to join a college team. The athletes themselves are also called recruits.

rivalry
An ongoing competition between two players or teams.

seed
A rank assigned to a player or team in a tournament.

triangle offense
A basketball strategy that focuses on spacing, cuts, and ball movement.

underdog
The person or team that is not expected to win.

MORE INFORMATION

BOOKS

Big Book of Who Women in Sports: The 101 Stars Every Fan Needs to Know. Triumph, 2025.

Giedd, Steph. *Basketball Strategies*. Abdo, 2024.

Hanlon, Luke. *Everything Basketball*. Abdo, 2025.

ONLINE RESOURCES

To learn more about iconic March Madness champions, please visit **abdobooklinks.com** or scan this QR code. These links are routinely monitored and updated to provide the most current information available.

INDEX

ABOUT THE AUTHOR

Charlie Beattie is a writer, editor, and former sportscaster. Originally from Saint Paul, Minnesota, he now lives in Charleston, South Carolina, with his wife and son.